More Cat Tales

by Rosemary Byers

Cats by Alice Carroll

Edited By: Dr. Robert Pace

© 1999 by Lee Roberts Music Publications, Inc.
International Copyright Secured.
ALL RIGHTS RESERVED.
Unauthorized copying, arranging, adapting, recording or
public performance is an infringement of copyright.
Infringers are liable under the law.

A Word to the *Student*... from the Cats of *More* Cat Tales

As a group we are humorous, charming and cute
And full of surprises which - if you're astute -
You'll dazzle your friends and even your teacher
with glorious grasp of each musical feature
(Which you have discovered and they can't dispute):

More Than Just A Pretty Face

Parallel majors and minors are here -
Sometimes apart and sometimes quite near.
Various meters from common to strange
And multiple keys (which of course you can change)
from four sharps to no sharps, and flats here and there.

Legatos, staccatos and slurs to "PURRfect."
Dynamics and triplets and grace notes connect
The music with Tales we hope will amuse,
As you learn all the musical tricks you can use
To show you're an expert in ev'ry respect!

(All modesty aside, of course)

MORE Cat Tales

Contents

Horace the Hungry Hunter	4
Stuffed Cat	6
Siamese Lullaby	7
Cat on a Hot Tin Roof	8
Bye, Bye, Birdie	10
Sour Puss	12
Fat Cat	13
Picnic in the Woods	14
Little Cat Lost	16
Cat Show!	18
Sore Loser	21
Alley Cat Spat	22

Horace The Hungry Hunter

(Yum, yum, eat 'em up!)

Stuffed Cat

Slow and queasy

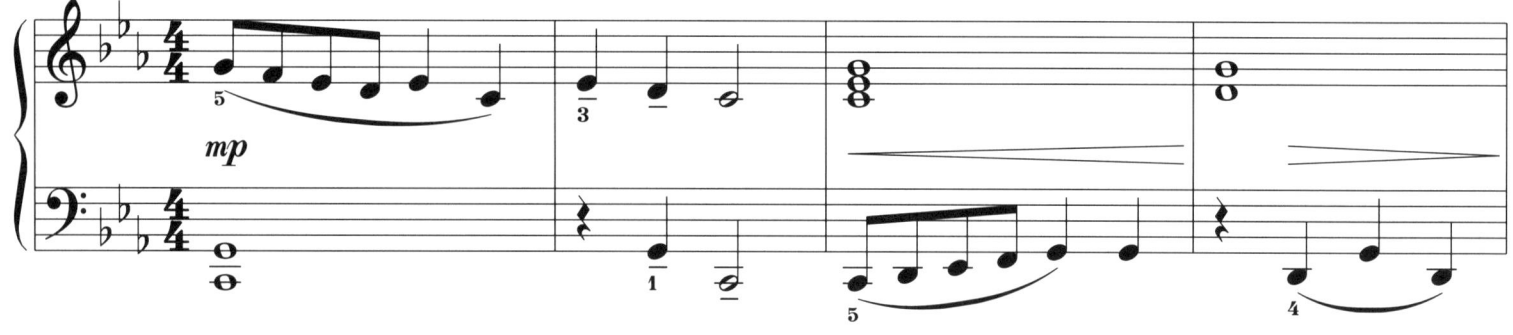
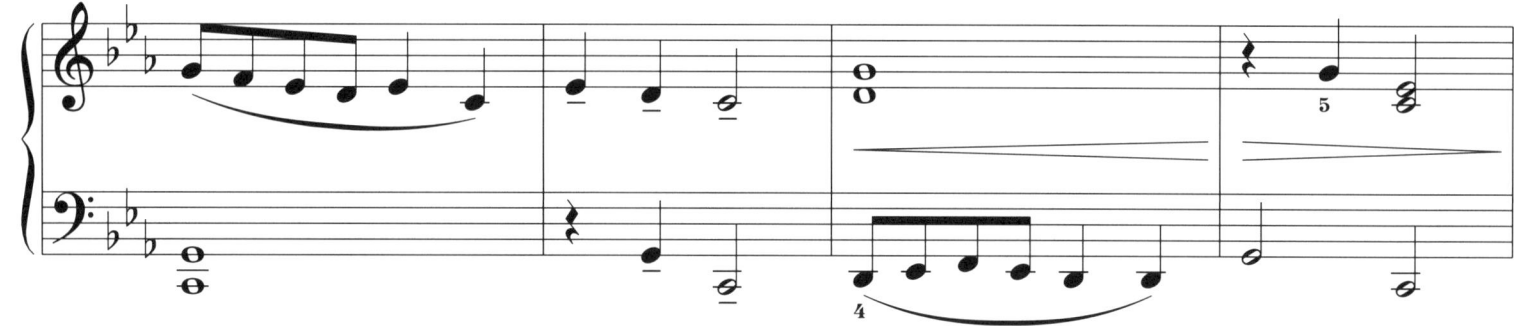

(Burp!)

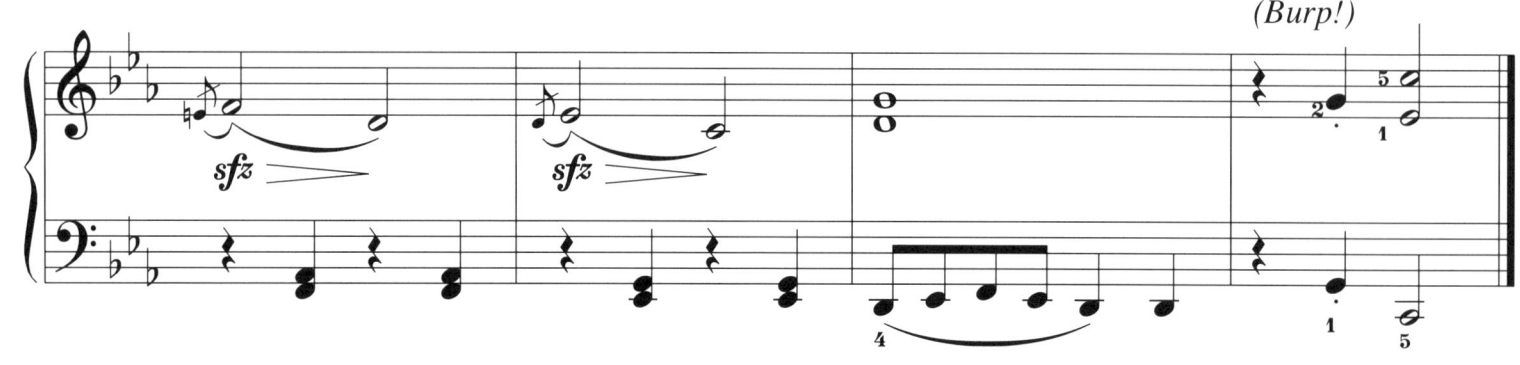

Siamese Lullaby

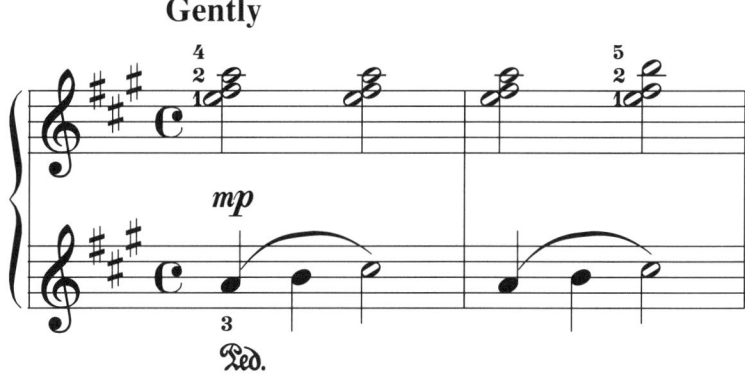

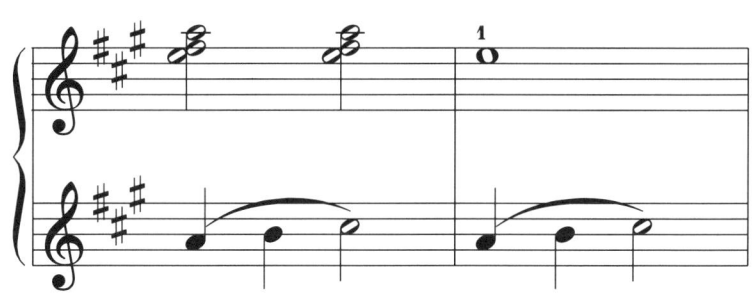

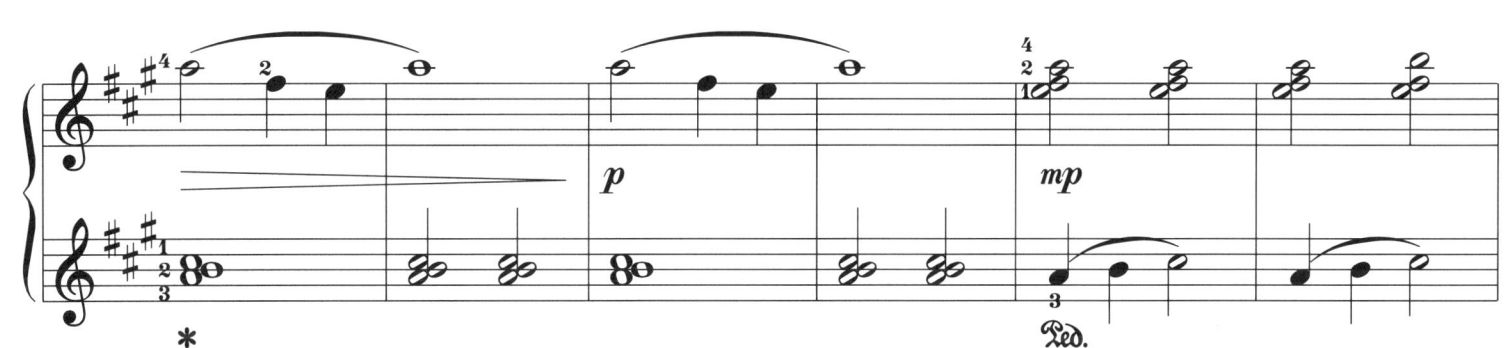

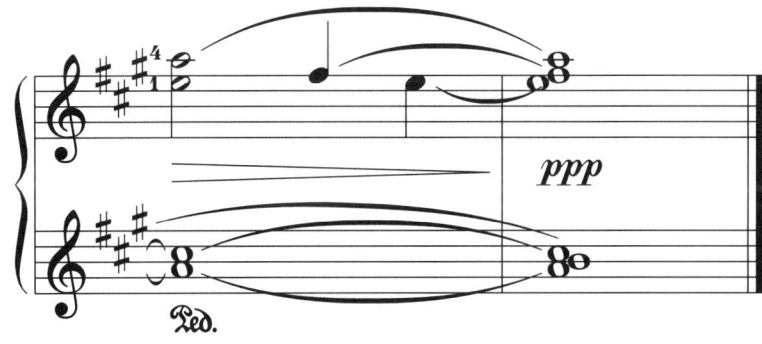

Cat on a Hot Tin Roof

Bye, Bye Birdie!

Fat Cat

Swaggering

Picnic in the Woods

Little Cat Lost

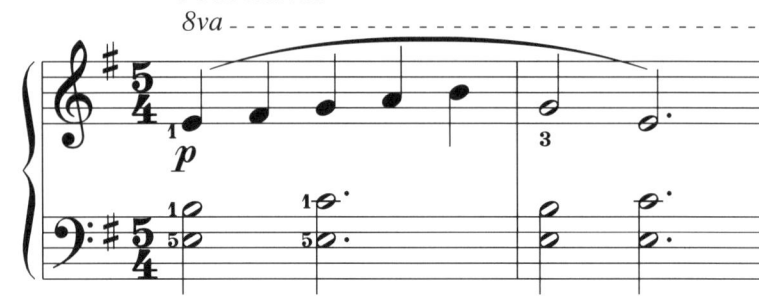

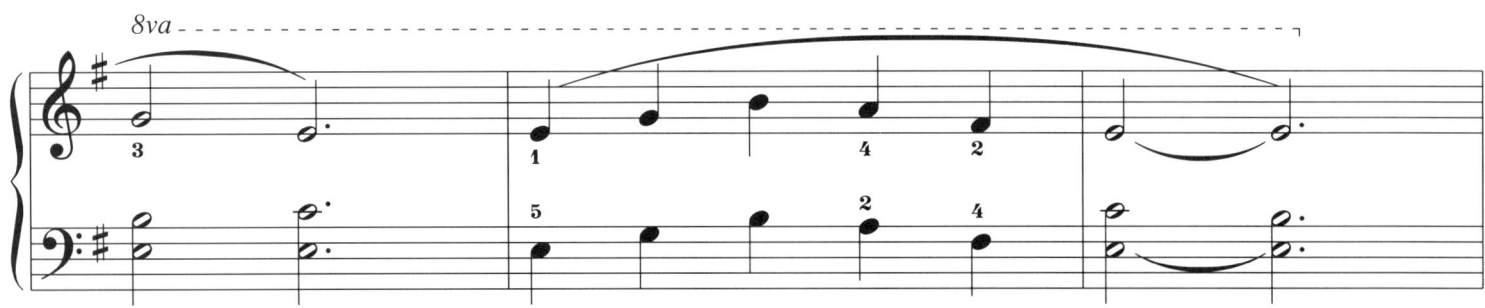

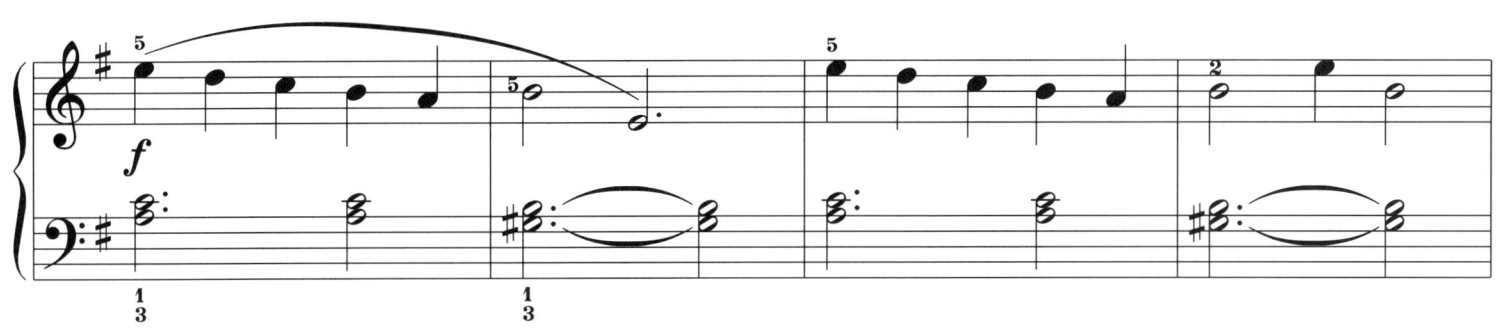

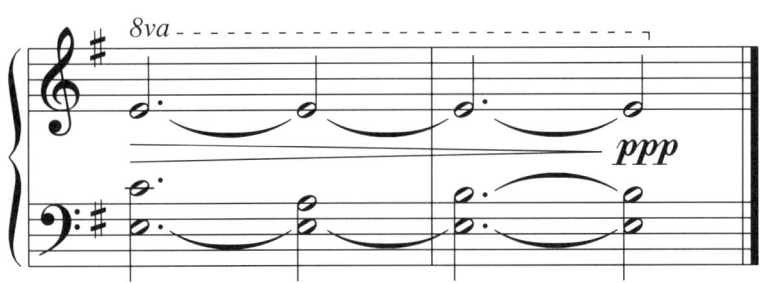

Cat Show

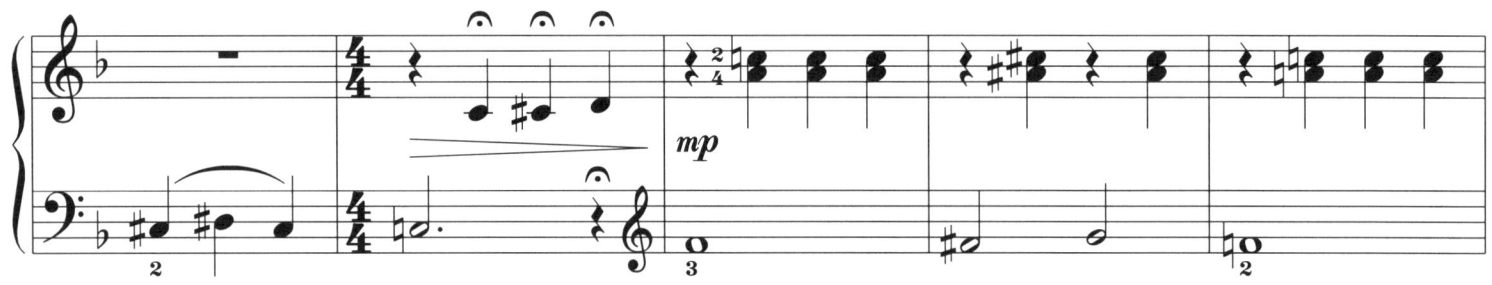

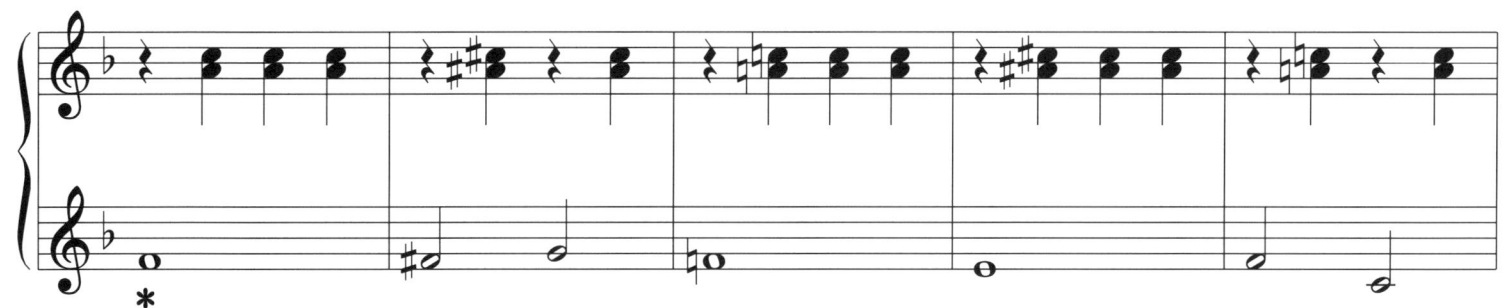

And the winner is…

poco accelerando

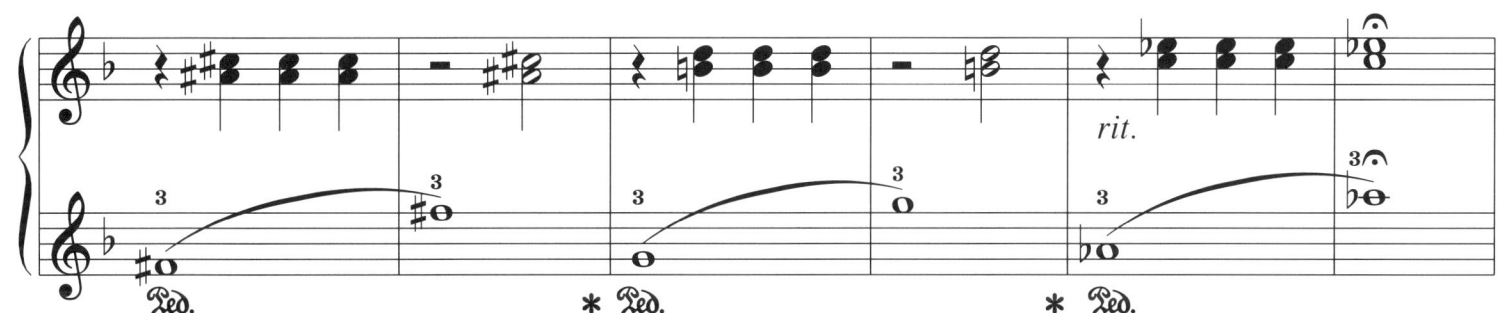

rit.

Sore Loser!

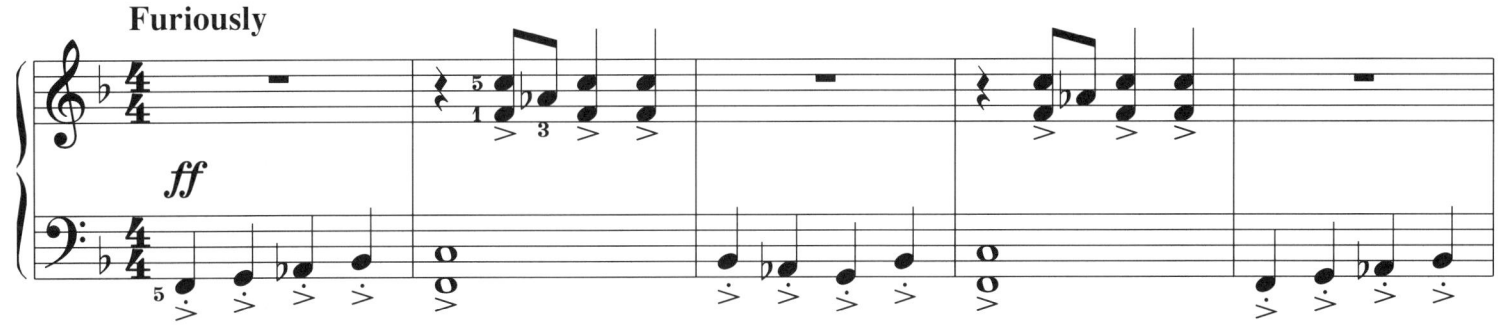

Alley Cat Spat

Fast and furious!

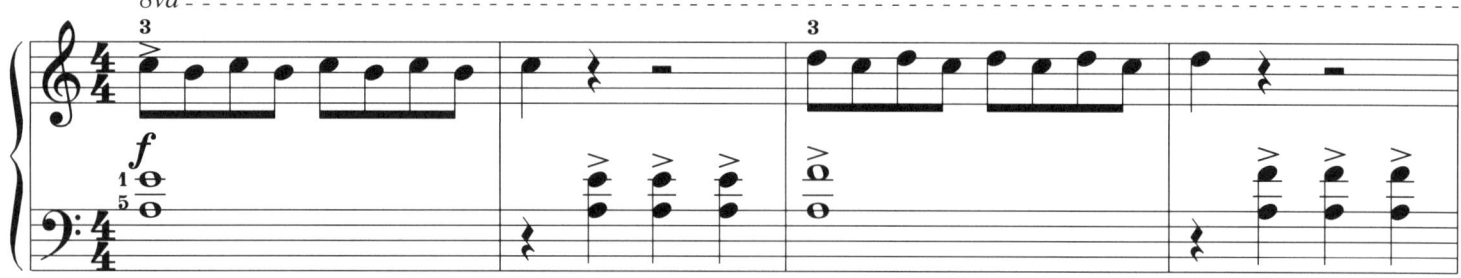

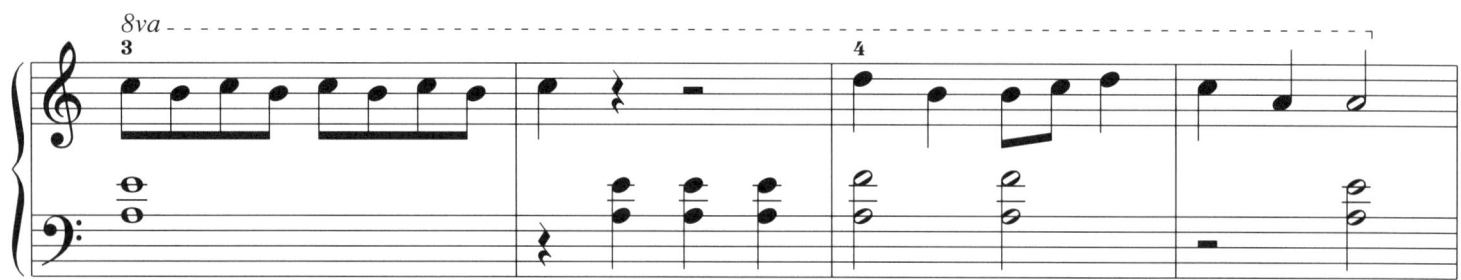

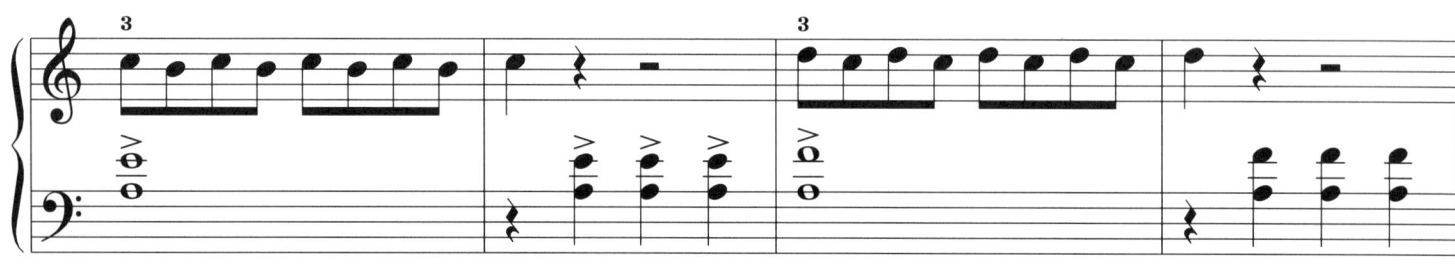

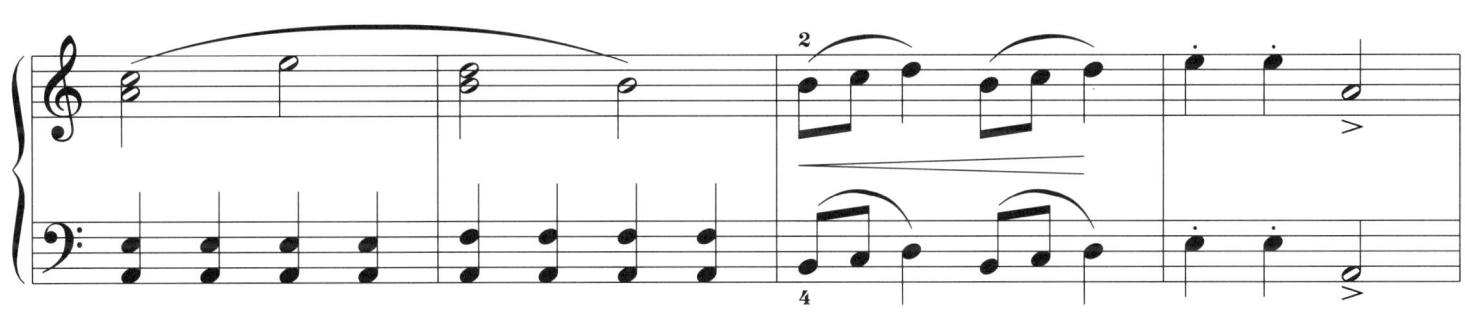

The End